VINTAGE VICTORIAN

Coloring The Victorian Era

KYLE SCHWOB

EFFECT
OF AN
OLD
STYLE
CORSET
THE
NEW
FIG-
URE

H. HARDCASTL
EST 1770
PAWNBROKE

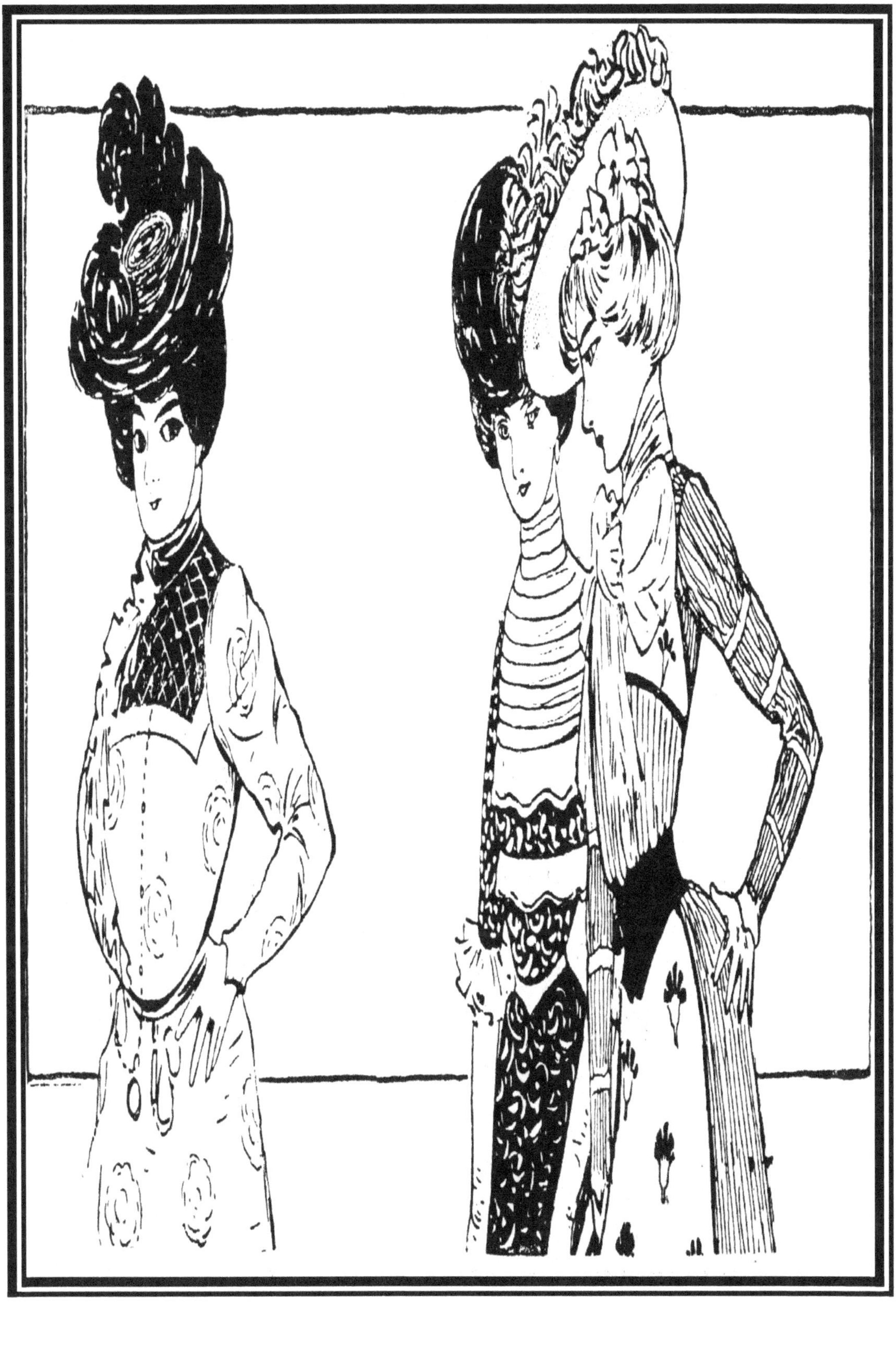

Test Your Colors Here!

www.ingramcontent.com/pod-product-compliance
Lightning Source LLC
Chambersburg PA
CBHW081140280526
45787CB00007B/3157
* 9 7 8 1 5 1 9 3 3 9 3 6 2 *